The Pennsylvania Colony

KEVIN CUNNINGHAM

Children's Press®
An Imprint of Scholastic Inc.
New York Toronto London Auckland Sydney
Mexico City New Delhi Hong Kong
Danbury, Connecticut

Content Consultant

Jeffrey D. Kaja, PhD
Assistant Professor of History
California State University, Northridge

Library of Congress Cataloging-in-Publication Data

Cunningham, Kevin, 1966–
  The Pennsylvania colony/Kevin Cunningham.
     p. cm.—(A true book)
  Includes bibliographical references and index.
  ISBN-13: 978-0-531-25396-0 (lib. bdg.)   ISBN-13: 978-0-531-26609-0 (pbk.)
  ISBN-10: 0-531-25396-1 (lib. bdg.)   ISBN-10: 0-531-26609-5 (pbk.)
  1. Pennsylvania—History—Colonial period, ca. 1600-1775—Juvenile literature. I. Title. II. Series.
  F152.C96 2011
  974.8'02—dc22   2011007148

All rights reserved. Published in 2012 by Children's Press, an imprint of Scholastic Inc.
Printed in China 62
SCHOLASTIC, CHILDREN'S PRESS, A TRUE BOOK, and associated logos are trademarks and/or registered trademarks of Scholastic Inc.
3 4 5 6 7 8 9 10 R 21 20 19 18 17 16 15 14 13

Find the Truth!

Everything you are about to read is true *except* for one of the sentences on this page.

Which one is **TRUE**?

T or F The Quakers influenced Pennsylvania's history.

T or F Pennsylvanians had peaceful relations with all Native Americans.

Find the answers in this book.

3

Contents

THE BIG TRUTH!

Philadelphians celebrate the reading of the Declaration of Independence.

Pennsylvania's Founding Fathers

The French and Indian War was one part of a war that took place in colonies around the world.

Timeline of Pennsylvania Colony History

10,000 BCE

Ancient Native Americans begin to settle in present-day Pennsylvania.

1609

Explorer Henry Hudson sails into Delaware Bay.

1682

The construction of Philadelphia begins.

1774

The First Continental Congress meets in Philadelphia.

1781

The British surrender to American colonists.

1790

Philadelphia becomes the temporary capital of the United States

First Nation

Several Native American groups had lived in Pennsylvania for centuries before Europeans came to colonize it. The Susquehannocks were an **Iroquois** people. They lived near the Susquehanna River. The Lenni-Lenape lived near the Delaware River and the Atlantic coast to the east. Lenni-Lenape means the "true people" in their language. They farmed, hunted, and fished. Their community was made up of about 20,000 people in 1600.

 After they were done farming in the fall, small groups of Lenni-Lenape moved to the woods to hunt.

The Lenni-Lenape lived in wigwams and longhouses in small villages. Wigwams were dome-shaped buildings of bark over a wooden frame. Longhouses were buildings about 30 to 110 feet (9 to 34 m) long and 20 feet (6 m) wide. Women took care of the home. They raised children, cooked meals, and made clothes from deerskins and furs. They also controlled the tribe's property and chose male chiefs to handle affairs with outsiders.

Lenni-Lenape women oversaw farms that grew maize (corn), squash, and other crops. Men hunted deer and turkeys with bows and short spears. They fished in rivers and along the ocean coast.

The Lenni-Lenape built longhouses in their farming communities.

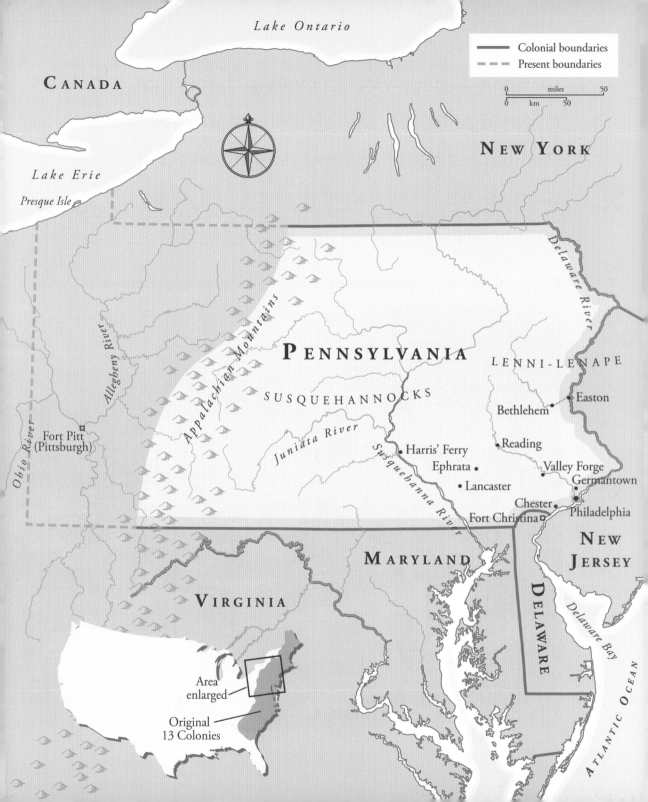

Lake Ontario

CANADA

Lake Erie

Presque Isle

NEW YORK

Colonial boundaries
Present boundaries

0   miles   50
0   km   50

Allegheny River

Ohio River

Fort Pitt
(Pittsburgh)

Appalachian Mountains

PENNSYLVANIA

SUSQUEHANNOCKS

Juniata River

Susquehanna River

LENNI-LENAPE

Delaware River

Bethlehem •   • Easton

• Reading

• Harris' Ferry
Ephrata •

• Valley Forge
Germantown

• Lancaster

Chester •

Fort Christina □   • Philadelphia

MARYLAND

NEW
JERSEY

VIRGINIA

DELAWARE

Delaware Bay

Area
enlarged

Original
13 Colonies

ATLANTIC OCEAN

Land of Plenty

English explorer Henry Hudson sailed his ship into Delaware Bay in 1609. Hudson worked for the Dutch East India Company. He was hired to find a water route that connected the Atlantic and Pacific Oceans. Hudson did not discover such a passage. But he found a land with a lot of rich soil, thick forests, and wild animals. He wrote to his employers in the Netherlands to tell them what he had found.

 Hudson River and Hudson Bay are named after Henry Hudson.

Fur trading was a major part of the European settlers' interactions with American Indians.

Hudson's discovery gave the Netherlands a quick start on settling the land around Delaware Bay. Dutch fur traders set up trading posts along the Delaware River at the bay's northern end. They offered the Lenni-Lenape goods such as metal knives and sturdy *duffel* cloth. In return, the traders received the furs of beaver and other animals that could be sold for a profit in Europe.

Settlers Arrive

Two ships from Sweden arrived in 1638 with Swedish and Finnish families. They planned to settle in the area. Their leader was Peter Minuit. Minuit had already served as governor of New Amsterdam, present-day New York City. He now worked for a company that wanted to establish a **colony** to sell valuable furs and tobacco.

Peter Minuit purchased Manhattan Island from the local natives for a very small sum of money.

Though he worked for the Swedish, Peter Minuit was Dutch.

New Sweden

The settlers built Fort Christina as a shelter in case of attack by Indians or other Europeans. They called their colony New Sweden. Some colonists traded for furs with friendly native groups. Others learned how to farm from the Lenni-Lenape. The settlers added maize, tomatoes, squash, and other native foods to their diets. Forests in the area provided the settlers with wood to build houses, make wooden farming tools, and heat their homes.

The fertile soil along the Delaware River made the settlers' farms a great success.

By 1655, about 500 settlers live in New Sweden.

New Sweden's location along the Delaware River made it a desirable location for colonization.

A Change of Rulers

New Sweden was a poor and small colony. It fell to the control of the Netherlands in 1655. English soldiers captured the colony nine years later without a fight. They told the small population of Dutch, Swedes, and Finns that they had become **subjects** of England. More English colonists soon arrived to join them. But it was the arrival of a new leader in 1682 that brought even greater changes.

William Penn

King Charles II gave Englishman William Penn a **charter** in 1681 that made him owner of the colony. The king named the colony Pennsylvania. This meant "Penn's Woods" in Latin. Penn planned to make Pennsylvania a place where people could freely practice their religion. This was not allowed in England. Penn called his plan "a holy experiment." He had been jailed years earlier for his Quaker religious beliefs in England.

In addition to Pennsylvania, Penn controlled the land that later became Delaware.

William Penn named Pennsylvania in honor of his father.

The Quakers

The Society of Friends, or Quakers, organized in the 1640s in England and Wales. Quakers held many ideas that were unpopular at the time. They believed God spoke directly to individuals. They also believed that people did not need **clergy** to communicate with God. Quakers thought that all people were spiritually equal.

William Penn encouraged good relationships with the local natives.

Penn's Leadership

Penn allowed the colonists to elect government representatives when he arrived in Pennsylvania in 1682. He also organized a treaty with the Lenni-Lenape promising fair treatment. Penn was inspired by Quaker teachings. He wrote the Frame of Government. The Frame was a **constitution** to govern the colony. It promised protection of property, fair trials and punishments, freedom to worship, and the right to disagree with government.

The colony began building a city in 1682 that Penn himself had planned. It was to be called Philadelphia, the Greek word for "city of brotherly love." Five thousand people lived in the city by 1697. The peaceful Quaker lifestyle at first made Philadelphia a quiet city. But the promise of religious freedom soon brought people of many different faiths from countries such as Germany and Wales. Twenty thousand people lived in Pennsylvania by 1700.

Today, Philadelphia is home to more than 1.5 million people.

Philadelphia grew to become a major port city.

Quakers valued education.

CHAPTER 3

Life as a Colonist

Quaker beliefs influenced life in early Pennsylvania. The Frame of Government proposed that children should learn to write by age 12. This was a worthy goal. Many adults in the 13 colonies were **illiterate**. Quakers believed in equality. Both girls and boys attended school. Children attended class for only part of the day. They spent the rest of their time doing chores. Boys learned their fathers' trades by working alongside them.

Quaker schools often consisted of a single classroom.

Farm work was difficult, but the rewards were great for the early German settlers.

On the Farm

Newcomers to the colony included German farmers. They were attracted by the good, cheap farmland. A new farmer often built a log cabin as his family's first home. He would usually build a larger home of stone and cut wood later. Food was stored in cool, earthen cellars. Farm animals were kept in barns. An entire community often gathered to raise a barn for a neighbor. It usually took them one or two days to do this.

Women raised the children and worked at family tasks such as preparing meals. German farm women introduced foods such as coleslaw, sausage, and waffles to the American diet. Women also spun wool into yarn. They mended and washed clothing. They also churned butter from milk and kept gardens. Boys did farm chores and worked in the fields.

Farm communities were centered around town squares.

About 65,000 Germans settled in Pennsylvania between 1727 and 1775.

Shoemaking was just one of the many trades practiced by men in Pennsylvania.

Shoes were often made of leather and wood during colonial times.

Working at a Trade

Farmers used iron-edged wooden tools. They cut crops with long blades. Pennsylvania's land was excellent for growing wheat. Farmers sold it throughout the American colonies. Many immigrants were skilled at crafts such as shoemaking, baking, ironworking, and tailoring. The products they sold allowed fellow colonists to buy cheaper local goods rather than pay high prices for items brought from England.

Westward expansion was a major part of life in North America during the 18th century.

Spreading West

The colonial government built roads after 1700 to connect Philadelphia with new villages such as Reading and Germantown. Fifty-foot-wide (15 meters) highways allowed travel for stagecoaches, mail carriers, and large Conestoga wagons full of farm goods. But the colonists crossed onto Native American villages and hunting grounds as they pushed west. William Penn's promise of fair treatment was being broken. So was the peace.

CHAPTER 4

Times of Trouble

New immigrants pushed the **frontier** westward as eastern Pennsylvania became more crowded. Farmers failed to sign treaties with Native Americans. They claimed land and defended it at all costs. Immigrants also began to settle on land near the Ohio River. This area was claimed by France, an enemy of Great Britain. The two countries were prepared to fight for control of North America by the 1750s.

 The French and Indian War was part of a larger European conflict known as the Seven Years' War.

French and Indian War

In April 1754, French soldiers drove off colonists building a fort at present-day Pittsburgh. A Virginia **militia** led by George Washington and supported by native Mingo warriors crushed a small French force the next month. British troops then lost a major battle. They partially retreated from the Pennsylvania frontier. Quaker officials opposed violence. But they realized the colony had to organize a militia to protect its western frontier.

George Washington gained important military experience during the French and Indian War.

Many militiamen lacked proper military training.

Pennsylvania's militiamen fought alongside British troops during the war.

War in Pennsylvania

The Pennsylvania militia attacked the pro-French Lenni-Lenape in April 1756 in their village of Kittanning. The militia lost more men than the Indians. But it burned down the village and rescued 11 American prisoners. The Pennsylvania militia later joined a British force that drove the French into present-day Canada. The French and Indian War ended in 1760 with France's defeat. Many Native Americans moved west after the loss of their French allies.

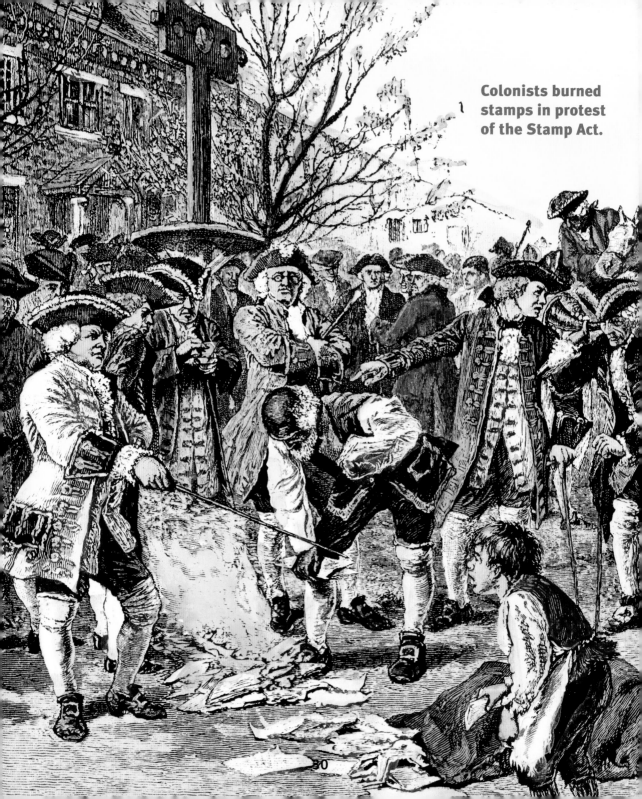

Colonists burned stamps in protest of the Stamp Act.

30

CHAPTER 5

The Fight for Independence

Great Britain imposed new taxes on the American colonists after the war. The taxes would help pay for the war and the frontier forts that defended the Americans. The Sugar Act of 1764 and the Stamp Act of 1765 greatly angered most colonists. They had no representation in the British government. They thought it was unfair for the British to force new laws or taxes on them. The colonists called it "taxation without representation."

Stamps were a common form of taxation in Great Britain.

Tea was a very popular drink among the colonists.

Taxes and Tea

Colonial leaders agreed to **boycott** British goods. Benjamin Franklin was a Philadelphia printer and inventor. He sailed to London to speak with British leaders. He warned them that the colonists would fight if the taxes did not stop. The British then put a tax on tea and allowed a British company to sell it tax-free in the colonies. The company could sell tea cheaply and put American tea sellers out of business.

There were 56 representatives at the First Continental Congress.

The First Continental Congress met at Carpenters' Hall in Philadelphia.

Decisions in Philadelphia

On September 5, 1774, the First Continental Congress met in Philadelphia to discuss the colonist's plans. Pennsylvania's six representatives at the Congress hoped to reach a peaceful understanding with Britain. But others voted to send a letter to King George III stating their complaints and asking for better treatment. The Congress also passed a new boycott against British products. They asked Americans not to sell goods to the British.

Early Defeats

The Second Continental Congress met in Philadelphia on May 10, 1775. Colonists had already fought the British in Boston by then. The American Revolutionary War had begun. The Congress asked each colony to raise troops for a Continental Army. George Washington was made commander-in-chief. Continentals had lost battles in New York and retreated to Pennsylvania by late 1776. Washington was defeated near Chester, Pennsylvania, in July 1777. The Continental Congress fled Philadelphia.

The Battles of Lexington and Concord started off the American Revolution.

General Washington's men received military training during their stay at Valley Forge.

Winter was harsh at Valley Forge.

The British thought they could end the war by capturing Philadelphia. The British army marched into the city in September 1777. But the Americans surprised the British by continuing to fight. Washington and his battered 12,000-man army set up winter quarters at nearby Valley Forge in December. The troops suffered from disease and a lack of food and warm clothing. But relief was on the way. France, the Netherlands, and Spain agreed to aid the Americans.

Benjamin Franklin

Benjamin Franklin was an author, scientist, inventor, and a leading statesman during American's fight for independence. In 1776, he was on the **committee** to draft the Declaration of Independence, the document that announced America's independence from Britain. Franklin spent from 1776 to 1785 in France building strong relations with the French. He argued against slavery and served as president of Pennsylvania's Constitutional Convention after his return.

Over 300 colonists were killed in the Battle of Wyoming.

Conflict between the colonists and the Native Americans was often brutally violent.

Frontier Battles

The British feared that the French navy might attack Philadelphia. They left the city in May 1778. The war shifted to the southern colonies. But in Pennsylvania, the Iroquois attacked American colonists on the western frontier. Iroquois and pro-British colonists wiped out the Pennsylvania militia in early July at the Battle of Wyoming. Frontier fighting continued until a brutal winter starved the Iroquois into stopping their attacks in 1780.

Pennsylvania's Founding Fathers

Getting the Declaration of Independence approved by the colonies was a difficult task for the Second Continental Congress. On July 1, 1776, nine of the 13 colonies voted to approve the declaration. But leaders at the Congress wanted every colony to support it to guarantee they would fight together against the British. Twelve colonies approved it on July 2. New York did not vote for or against. Nine Pennsylvanian representatives signed the declaration, including the following three men.

Robert Morris

Robert Morris was a successful trader. He voted against the declaration on July 1. But he later signed it and lent money to the Continental army. He became head of the Continental navy and a U.S. senator after the war.

Benjamin Rush

Benjamin Rush was a physician and professor. He served for a short time as surgeon general in the Continental army. He was a fierce opponent of George Washington, a position he later regretted. Rush became the United States's most famous physician after the Revolutionary War.

John Dickinson

John Dickinson wrote influential papers with Thomas Jefferson for the Continental Congress. He opposed an American declaration of independence at the time. But he later served in the militia. He was elected president of Pennsylvania after the war.

Mad Anthony Wayne leads his troops into battle at Stony Point.

Fighting and Winning

Pennsylvania troops and militia served with the Continental army all across the colonies. Pennsylvanian Anthony Wayne was called Mad Anthony for his daring fighting style. He commanded Continentals in several battles. He personally led his men against a British fort at Stony Point, New York, in 1779. Pennsylvanian tradesmen made cannons and guns. Craftsmen provided shoes and tools. Farmers helped feed the Continental army with food grown on Pennsylvania soil.

The Americans eventually defeated their enemy. The main British army surrendered in 1781. Fighting continued for several months. On September 3, 1783, British and American leaders signed the Treaty of Paris. This ended the conflict. The price of independence came at a high cost. Warfare had destroyed much of the Pennsylvania frontier. Trade suffered in Philadelphia. American Patriots often turned violently against their pro-British neighbors.

Those loyal to Britain were sometimes beaten, killed, or forced out of town.

The Second State

Pennsylvania sent eight representatives to a convention to discuss a constitution for the new nation in May 1787. The 13 colonies voted upon the proposed document after months of work. Pennsylvania agreed to the new U.S. Constitution and became the second state in the union on December 12, 1787. Philadelphia served as the U.S. capital from 1790 to 1800. It was an appropriate honor for a city, state, and colony that had done so much to advance the cause of independence. ★

The Constitution is the foundation of the modern U.S. government.

There were 55 representatives at the Constitutional Convention.

Population of Lenni-Lenape in 1600: About 20,000

Population of Philadelphia in 1697: 5,000

Population of Pennsylvania in 1700: 20,000

Width of Pennsylvania's colonial highways: 50 ft. (15 m)

Number of settlers rescued at Battle of Kittanning: 11

Number of Pennsylvania representatives at First Continental Congress: 6

Number of Pennsylvanians who signed the Declaration of Independence: 9

Number of Continental army soldiers at Valley Forge: 12,000

Number of years Philadelphia served as U.S. capital: 10

Did you find the truth?

T The Quakers influenced Pennsylvania's history.

F Pennsylvanians had peaceful relations with all Native Americans.

Resources

Books

Dalton, Anne. *The Lenape of Pennsylvania, New Jersey, New York, Delaware, Wisconsin, Oklahoma, and Ontario*. New York: PowerKids, 2005.

Gunderson, Jessica S. *The Second Continental Congress*. Mankato, MN: Compass Point, 2008.

Heinrichs, Ann. *Pennsylvania*. Mankato, MN: Compass Point, 2003.

Hinman, Bonnie. *William Penn*. Hockessin, DE: Mitchell Lane, 2006.

Hintz, Martin. *The Pennsylvania Colony*. Mankato, MN: Capstone, 2006.

Landau, Elaine. *The Declaration of Independence*. New York: Children's Press, 2008.

Levy, Janey. *William Penn: Shaping a Nation*. New York: Rosen Classroom, 2009.

Somervill, Barbara A. *Pennsylvania*. New York: Children's Press, 2009.

Organizations and Web Sites

The Delaware Nation

www.delawarenation.com

Learn about the history of Delaware's Native American peoples, and see what is happening in the Delaware/ Lenni-Lenape Nation today.

The State Museum of Pennsylvania

www.statemuseumpa.org

View online exhibits that detail the lives of the Lenni-Lenape, colonial history, and more.

Places to Visit

Independence National Historical Park

143 S. Third Street
Philadelphia, PA 19106
(215) 597-8787
www.nps.gov/inde/index.htm
Visit the heart of historic Philadelphia and see where Patriots signed the Declaration of Independence and discussed the Constitution.

Valley Forge National Historical Park

1400 North Outer Line Drive
King of Prussia, PA 19406
(610) 783-1099
www.nps.gov/vafo/index.htm
Walk where George Washington and the Continental army camped during the winter of 1777–1778.

Important Words

boycott (BOI-kaht)—refusing to buy goods from a person, group, or country

charter (CHAHR-tur)—a formal document guaranteeing rights or privileges

clergy (KLUR-jee)—people trained to lead religious groups

colony (KAH-luh-nee)—an area settled by people from another country and controlled by that country

committee (ke-MI-tee)—a group assigned a special task or duty

constitution (kahn-sti-TOO-shun)—the laws of a country that state the rights of the people and the powers of government

frontier fruhn-TEER)—the far edge of a settled territory or country

illiterate (i-LIT-ur-it)—unable to read or write

Iroquois (IR-ih-kwoi)—a group of Native American peoples that included the Susquehannocks and Mohawks (but not the Lenni-Lenape)

militia (muh-LISH-uh)—a group of people who are trained to fight but who aren't professional soldiers

subjects (SUB-jekts)—people who live in a kingdom or under the authority of a king or queen

Index

Page numbers in **bold** indicate illustrations

About the Author

Kevin Cunningham has written more than 40 books on disasters, the history of disease, Native Americans, and other topics. Cunningham lives near Chicago with his wife and young daughter.